The New
Atlantis
&
The Sophia
Codex

Blanca Beyar

DEDICATION

To all the brave souls who dared to become
part of the earth experience! Through the many lifetimes
that you have traveled to experience, to remember and
to achieve your purpose, this book is dedicated to you.

ACKNOWLEDGMENTS

As it is a divine truth that no one ever accomplishes anything on their own, my deepest gratitude must be expressed to Maia Chrystine Nartoomid for the incredible and sacred guidance she provides as an Elder Akashic Translator. Your devotion and wisdom have truly provided me with validation and support. Thank you!
I am deeply grateful to Drunvalo Melchizedek, for the decades of teachings and insight you have offered humanity, of which also guided me in indescribable ways! And to my complimentary partner, Robert Cochise, I am eternally grateful for the great dedication placed in assisting me to bring life to the scribbles of the sacred Sophia Codex. You placed your signature and loving energy into each symbol and for this, I am forever grateful to you. I love you!

Great Apocalypse

The Great Apocalypse is here. In this epic time of our existence, we are collectively and universally living in the great Apocalyptic times spoken of throughout existence, in worldwide religious and spiritual beliefs. We are——more than ever——being invited to awaken to the "*Great Unveiling of Truth.*" Thus, the great Apocalypse is indeed a triumph arrival to the "moment" of our existence where we can finally awaken from the illusion of spiritual amnesia and step in to claim our victory in having reached a state of universal conscious awareness. This is the Great Awakening. This is The Great Apocalypse.

As we witness the crumbling and dismantling of the world as we have never seen before, it is only natural to allow fears to take grip of our minds and souls. For, how can distortion, confusion, fear, control, and separation be a representation of a New World? And as we continue to encounter the fall of a humanity, we secretly ask ourselves if this may indeed be the end of the world that many scribes and sacred texts prophesized thousands of years ago for the future of our earth. Are we living in the end times?

The Great Apocalypse is here, and we are indeed witnessing the end of days of an old paradigm world. The Great Reveal and Awakening is the doorway that reveals the entry into the New Paradigm, the New Earth. The world is not going to obliterate out of existence or explode into the abyss. The Earth, is however, in the process of anchoring celestial, higher vibration energies that will uphold the establishment of the New Earth frequencies. This is the ascension process.

There is no denying that if we turn to biblical scriptures and sacred texts, we will see the evidence of the "**Four Horsemen,**" spoken in the Book of Revelations as well as the prophecies in the book of Ezekiel consuming and encircling the world: *Conquest, war, famine, and death.* These prophecies were not intended to lead us into a state of fearful paralysis, to believe in a punishing "God" or to experience the suppression of a world stripped of spiritual soul freedom. The parables of these ancient texts were written so that we could identify and recognize when the time of the Great Awakening was upon us!

As a Humanity, we are at the threshold of proclaiming and executing the greatest conscious choice of our existence. There are two choices and they are in opposing polarities; One choice is to succumb to perpetual and ravaging fear and control that is consuming the old paradigm reality; **(Conquest),** you participate in the continuation of advocating and justifying separation and conflict **(War),** you grow weary by the mass consciousness creation of fear and indifference; you feel defeated, you are starving for freedom and unification, **(Famine),** and you begin to slowly lower your inspiration to live a joyful, purposeful and love-filled life; you begin to dwindle into a withered flower void of beauty and promise (**Death**).

Over the last decade, and gravely over the last three years, the world has witnessed a devastating and dramatic upheaval of indifferences amongst nations, communities, and people, which has provoked unparallel protests, conflicts and separation of a world divided. In an attempt to have a voice for justice, the human collective has fallen into the energies of Conquest and War, defeat through control, violence, judgment, separation and fear.

The onset of these protests quickly escalated as never before seen, to other factions of the world, which abided the mockery and disrespect of institutions and governments which once held a place of integrity and respect in the eyes of a society. Parties of opposing sides crossing incompressible boundaries for conquest. Institutions within mainstream media no longer committed to delivering noteworthy news with integrity, but deliberately taking sides to create greater havoc and war within society.

And nearly two years ago, the entire world became paralyzed when pestilence came knocking on the door and completely upturned the lives of a humanity forever. A great famine of human and spiritual freedom has seized the world as the ordinary practices that we took for granted have been taken away; no longer able to enjoy the simplicity of interactions with others, of the importance of sharing hugs and smiles with those that we love, of feeling the freedom of our existence and partaking in the experiences of life.

Yes, humanity has indeed entered the last phase of the Great Apocalypse and the presence of the last Horseman is blatantly striking at the will of souls who are desperately trying to maintain a sense of hope, a sense of faith and of sanity as the world around them continues to dismantle into an abyss of darkness and despair.

There is another choice that humanity can make. The execution of this other choice will require courage, faith and a steadfast will power from within each person to remember the true essence of their soul. It will require for each soul to recognize that the Great Apocalypse is a time of unveiling the divine truth of the illusion the mass consciousness has been living and an opportunity to step in to claim our sovereignty as celestial beings so that we can forge ahead to the *New Earth Paradigm*.

The choice to awaken to our divine truth and to embrace the roadmap that we have traveled throughout lifetimes and cycles to arrive to this epic juncture of our universal awakening is here for the taking. The time is now *Beloveds*, and when you allow yourselves to remember this, this realization of truth will carry you through the threshold, and past the illusions of the old paradigm world. This realization will unveil not only your divine truth, but it will also usher you through the gateway of spiritual liberation so that you can begin to experience the joys and freedom of the New Atlantis, the New Earth.

The most critical and important question of the moment, beloveds, is "Where is your focus and attention?" Are you willing and ready to move beyond the four horsemen upheaval that is intensely prevalent in the old paradigm so that you can proceed vibrationally into the new paradigm Earth?

The time is now.

The Rise of Atlantis

Throughout the ages, great speculation has surrounded the existence and validity of Atlantis. Were the Atlanteans a real civilization or were they mythical in nature and a fabrication of dreamers from a past world? A great many documentaries, television shows and books have been written about the Atlanteans, but none provide greater authentication than the manuscripts and books left by the beloved Edgar Cayce, the "Sleeping Seer." In his readings, Edgar shares great details about the civilization of Atlantis, of their highly advanced evolution as a species, its inhabitants, and its geographical location.

Indeed, Atlantis was not only a real civilization; they also play a crucial and vital role in the ascension of the New Earth Creation in our present timeline. For, it was the Atlanteans, who traveled through time into the future, and who came here to earth to secure the energetic frequencies of their own established evolution in a time capsule for a future release prior to the destruction of Atlantis.

Resembling the infiltration which the current old paradigm world has been experiencing here on earth, the Atlantean civilization, at the height of their incredible ascension, were infiltrated and compromised. In awareness that the compromise had created a distortion in the energetic field of their existence, the Atlanteans formulated a master plan that would play out in this current timeline of our earthly experience as a collective.

In many ways, although it may be difficult to fathom, the timelines of eons past and the situation of the Earth over the last several years have mirrored each other in ways that can be mind-jolting. And from a cosmic, energetic, and tine-line perspective, these two crucial existence points had to mirror each other up to this point in the old paradigm (earth) to provide the "fall of Atlantis" with another opportunity and outcome, "The Rise of Atlantis" in our earthly timeline today!

As a further confirmation to authenticate this revelation, we can also turn to the sacred writings, "The Emerald Green Tablets" written by the beloved Thoth, the Atlantean. In the works of the tablets, the initiate who can "hear" will recognize that Thoth is not only revealing the accounts and unfolding during the fall of Atlantis thousands of years ago; he is also fore warning the initiates of prophecy for futuristic events that will mirror the fall of

Atlantis—but which would have triumph results leading to the Earth's/Atlantis ascension. This revelation is unfolding and undertaking in our current world, between the Old Paradigm and the New Earth.

The fulfillment of a great, advanced civilization, which also possessed their divine attributes as celestial beings would not be lost but instead, laid to rest for a millennium of time so that at the appropriate "time" where their reality and the earth's pathway of awakening would be in alignment to merge and become One, they would *Rise* in unison.

The time capsule that was preserved through timelines contained the energetic encodement of the original blueprint and DNA composite of the advanced civilization of Atlantis. A contained "vessel "with a very specific element structure had to be found within the future timelines which would be capable of energetically storing the encodement for the future. Great *Shamans* of Atlantis knew that they could time-travel through energetic shamanic journeying to secure the encodement in a structure vessel for the future. As they traveled through the future, a perfect structure was found that could sustain and hold the encodement; the structure was no other than the *Statue of Liberty,* located in New York City.

One may ask, why not the Eiffel Towers, or the Giza in great Egypt or one of the many monuments of great importance around the world? The Statue of Liberty not only contained the precise elemental and physical structure to retain the encodement; the Lady Liberty also upheld the literal symbolic meaning that would complement the resonance and energy of the Atlantean encodement. The location of the Statue would also play a vital role, as

New York City has played a vital role in the world as the Capital of "Freedom and Strength" for centuries but not so ironically, has now also played a role in the collapse and fall of the very principles it was reverenced and admired for.

Thus, it is critically vital to emphasize that as the fall of a great Capital and of a world continues to prevail in this current timeline of the old paradigm, there is also an uprise and establishment taking place in the new paradigm Earth.

The release of the energetic encodement of Atlantis has successfully been released and anchored. The blueprint of the new Earth has been held in the DNA structure of many ascended souls who came here to hold the memory for the future new earth. This conglomerate of souls can be identified as the 144,000 who are spoken of in countless sacred texts and mystery teachings.

These "Warriors of the Light" have been present throughout lifetimes, upholding the torch of remembrance, of healing and of unification for many timelines throughout existence. These "Ascended Ones" can also be recognized in today's timeline as the "Lighthouses" who continue to shine the light and to guide the way out of darkness and into the light amidst the Apocalypse in the world today.

It is not a question of whether the "Light" will succeed in overcoming the "Dark" or whether the "Light" will be triumph in establishing the new Earth. The Light (the new Consciousness) has prevailed and succeeded; the new Earth has ascended to a higher vibrational field and the new paradigm within the new Earth is being constructed and developed already by the ascended souls who have been capable to uphold the new energetic frequencies of a 5th dimensional field and beyond.

The time has truly arrived for each of you to wake up from the sleep-state of the 3rd dimensional experience of limitation and smallness. The environment and matrix of the old paradigm has served its purpose and it provided you with the necessary experiences that were geared to commence your evolution and growth to a higher, divine potential; as it is not only your birthright, but also encoded in your DNA.

The new earth has risen and with this joyous achievement, it is your turn to also raise your vibration out of the old paradigm matrix. Your existence never intended to remain asleep or stuck in the old paradigm matrix. You inherently proposed to rise above the illusions and to reclaim your divine identity as a crystalized and evolved sentient being. Your DNA contains the molecules of the evolved Atlanteans. You are all part of the star seeds who came to earth to be part of the galactic and cosmic evolution of consciousness. Your divine potential is much grander and greater than you can ever imagine!

It is time to rise beloved ones. It is time to wake up!

The Second Coming

From the time of Christ's existence, we can witness how the control of the world was ignited by those in power; those who reconstructed through force the foundation of how society would live. A great reform took place during Christ's time that gave way to the rise of patriarchy, control, and the overtaking of humanity by the masculine energies through aggression, deceit, and manipulation. In many ways, this time era was truly the beginning of the "end" of a free society as well as the disconnection to the feminine aspect of our divine essence.

Christ was a supreme and beloved teacher, avatar, and messenger for the world and in his teachings, he often spoke of the "second coming of a new kingdom." This "promise" that Christ prophesized would become the foundation of hope for millions of hopeful and faithful followers around the world, and rightfully so.

Many believe(d), even today, that the echoing of these sacred words was a promise that the Christ himself was speaking of his return; a return which would insure an end to the cycle of humanity's demise, separation, and suffering. It was a promise that gave hope to the ending to the ruling of the patriarchal dominion upon the world.

Christ spoke truth when he taught in saying that the "Kingdom of God is within us." We all possess the Universal Life Force seed within our very makeup; we have simply forgotten and through this forgetfulness, have handed our awakening to eternal forces, rather than going within to activate our own divine essence.

The second coming was a promise that in a time, the earth and humanity would find themselves in the perfect "time" to awaken to their truth and to advance themselves beyond a 3-dimensional consciousness, to a higher vibrational and divine space of awareness. YOU are the second coming! There is no one to wait for; you have been waiting for your sacred self to realize this, to accept this, and to shift yourself into becoming the highest version of your divine expression.

The time has arrived for you to stop wondering how the world is going to change from the chaos and separation that has been created by the ones who "sleep" and those who have an agenda to keep the consciousness in a state of amnesia. The time is now, to realize that you have the power and the ability to create a shift so massive within yourself, that will also create a huge contribution to the rest of the world.

The change begins when you are ready to step away from the illusions of what you thought was truth, what others have created as truth, and to delve in deeply into your soul heart center to discover the truth. You are the promise that Christ and many other avatars have spoken of in prophecy. You hold the key to ignite a transformation within yourself and then to share that transformation with others by the very essence of your being-ness and example.

You are the second coming!

The Sophia Energy

The earth and humanity are ready to shift their existence reality from a dark state of separation, of ignorance and denial of the vibration of love, to a new world that is sustained on the principles of unity, of compassion and love. The Sophia energy is the principality who is ushering and building the foundation for the new paradigm earth. The Sophia energy is the embodiment of the feminine aspect of the divine Life Force creation and as such, creation and intention are given birth to from the maternal womb of the mother archetype. The Sophia energy in the 5th dimensional space and beyond, will lead *her* children to a new oasis of paradise through the maternal soul heart center, which is the cornerstone of pure love. And in the energy of pure love, the *children* will have the freedom to truly express themselves without fear of judgment or ridicule, they will have the opportunity to discover and explore their hidden attributes and creative abilities which will enable them to create new visions and landscapes that will manifest into grander experiences and fulfillment in the new earth paradigm.

The Sophia energy of the new earth will usher in the next wave of humanity; the Crystal and Rainbow children who are comprised of highly enlightened star seeds from higher dimensional realms, who will become the ambassadors for the continued evolution of the new humanity and the new earth. The presence, energy and contribution of the star seeds will further assist in the cultivation and establishment of the Sophia codex; a new world which is founded on cooperation, unity, equality on all levels of existence, integrity, and accountability for the manifestation of individualized creation; collective consciousness when executing creation, observing the *whole* as opposed to the individualized *one*.

Although there will still be opportunities for soul growth in the new earth, choices will not be executed from a state of fear or from a state of unconsciousness, and as such, challenges will be viewed as they should be--opportunities for greater awareness and the ability to have reverence for the execution of thoughts and actions. The new humanity will learn how to master their consciousness, and this will joyfully insure the cultivation of a harmonious foundation within the new world paradigm.

The humanity of the old paradigm existence has endured enough suffering and limitations through the energies, influence, and control of the masculine archetype. The masculine energies are not gender, but specifically, a field of lower consciousness which exists within both genders in humanity. There has been a time and a place for the unfolding of these energies; and this place has been the 3rd dimensional field within the old paradigm earth. As a reality field, created by the mass consciousness, it is a real plane of existence within the reality of perception for every being, as well as the whole.

Yet, as the existence of a distorted reality is factual in the consciousness of the many, the new earth paradigm is also a collective reality that must be held in the highest level of perception for the conception of the new earth to fully develop in its cultivation and anchoring. The Sophia energy is reigning over the new earth paradigm and leading the warriors of the light as they establish the pillars of the new earth foundation through their own example and reflection of being the new collective consciousness and pioneers for the new earth!

Perhaps, the foretelling of these revelations may seem far reached within your current perception of reality, as so much dismantling and chaotic energies are surely in existence in the hemisphere of the old paradigm earth. The purpose of this sacred codex is to bring you into awareness that you have reached a conscious state of readiness to make a choice. The highest choice that you can make today is to shift your reality; to raise your vibration through the soul heart center so that you can begin to experience and to live in the new earth frequencies. The new earth is a real plane of existence, but it is also a vibrational state of consciousness. To experience the full spectrum of the frequencies of the new earth, you must consciously choose to change the internal channel of where you are placing your attention on. You must recognize that you have been tuned in to a channel which is akin to a controlled matrix of distortion and mind control.

Once you succeed in recognizing the mechanics of the controlled matrix, you can consciously choose to change the channel; to raise your vibration and to "tune in" to a higher level of reception. The Sophia energy and the principles of the Sophia codex are the foundation and frequency of the new paradigm, and the Sophia feminine aspect will assist you in reaching and to hold a higher state of vibration through the penetration of the soul heart center. All that is required is for you to surrender to the unveiling of your true heart. Relish in the release of all that you have completed and experienced in the old paradigm; be willing to honor and to have gratitude for every single step of the totality of your journey in the old earth. Allow yourself to see the gifts and opportunity for growth in every experience. Be willing to honor the sovereignty of each soul who is walking in their own and unique experience; void of judgment or superiority in a perception that you are at you may possess. greater wisdom by the awareness that you have. Be mindful that in the highest state of the *Absolute,* you are all *one.*

Now, as you prepare to receive the activations of the Sophia codex, remember that the introduction to the sacred symbols are much more than an illustration of lines and circles; the codex is a language of sacred geometry, which contain a high vibrational tuning and calibration. The codex is already embedded within the cellular aspect of your divine structure, genetically placed in your sacred DNA. The codex is a living vibration within your energy field and in this epic time of ascension in the new earth plane, the signature within your soul is eager and ready to become awaken to it true and higher vibrational state of divine consciousness. You are part of the collective Christ consciousness soul family who courageously volunteered to be the ambassadors for the new earth and the holders of the Sophia energy and codex.

There is a new star in the realm of the galactic field, and *she* is known as the **New Earth.** *She* shines brightly and proudly as the warriors of the light assist *her* in establishing a new foundation for the children of the earth as they celebrate their arrival to a new paradise. May you enjoy of *her* fruits and be blessed as you join *her* in creating your greatest manifestations yet, for all of creation in all the realities of existence!

The Sophia Codex

The Sophia Codex is a beautiful blueprint of the principles by which the New Earth is founded on an energetic and etheric level. The codes and their representations are the pillars that will uphold the creation and the flourishing of the New Earth. The gift of the codex was birthed from the Divine Mother Sophia as she held the vision of a new paradigm where her children will reign in the highest state of joy and unification. The containment of the Codex was held in sacred space in the inner world for thousands of years as a perfect hologram for the matrix of the New Earth. Once the vision was awakened and received by the

Goddess Sophia, the Codex was released into the womb of the Mother Earth as sacred fertilized eggs of divine intention to bring forth the birthing of the principles of the New Paradigm Earth.

The Sophia Codex upholds a similar energetic structure that can be compared to the Ten Commandments in Biblical scriptures as well as the Emerald Green Tablets of Thoth. In the forementioned, the by-laws, teachings and principles laid out were intended to illustrate how humanity could obtain a richer and fulfilled level of conscious living by adapting the teachings or principles. In simpler terms, the teachings and structures were intended to be a pathway that would lead to wholesome living based on the energetic principles held by the teachings as well as the protocols of the Mother Earth field.

The New Earth paradigm has ascended to a higher vibrational state of frequency and as such, all that resides within the container or field of the New Earth must match in frequency to reside within the field. In this manner, there is no internal inclusion or exclusion beloveds. Each individual aspect of the Divine within each soul must then truly choose to raise their vibration and frequency to "qualify themselves" into the New Paradigm field. This is truly the definition of the Ascension process. Not only does the New Earth reach a new level of consciousness and frequency, but also, all the inhabitants within the Earth. The alignment with the new level of consciousness promotes continued growth and expansion beyond the fifth dimension and it also ensures that denser energies do not interfere with the progression of the pathway back to higher consciousness in the New Earth.

The Sophia Codex is the matrix of the New Earth and carries the pure tone-vibration for the frequency of the soul's heart center. In the old paradigm, humanity primarily experienced life through the hologram of physicality and the "human heart." The ability to experience from the physical heart allowed humanity to experience the full spectrum of emotions and feelings but also added the component of filtering those expressions through a physical heart chamber (hurt, emotional injury, resentment, separation, hatred, etc.). All served a purpose in that the experiences of separation and detachment from the true heart center was a vehicle to bring an awareness to your true identity; the experiences of emotional distress were a catalyst to invoke a higher state of consciousness and to navigate you into the heart center of your soul.

The Sophia Codex is a divine blueprint that

defines and paves the way for the ascended soul to beautifully align with the new vibrational frequencies of the New Earth. This pathway is primarily directed by the vibration of the "Soul" heart center. Awakening now to a new level of consciousness of the divine self, the field of the new Earth create and hold the principles and foundation for a new experience of existence on a higher plane of creation, of manifestation, of awareness, of consciousness and of experience. In essence, the Sophia Codex is the New Language of the new paradigm but also, the new language of the soul in its higher existence of divine awareness!

The Sophia Codex is the "Key" (language) that cracks open the cylinders of the soul heart center and allows the frequencies of divine freedom, of pure love and divine consciousness to penetrate through the soul center as a release of remembrance, because the soul is already unconditional love and purity. It is important to recognize that it is not the soul that is being transformed; what is being transformed (upgraded) is the state of consciousness (your awareness) and, the plane field in which you play out the realization of your new consciousness (the new paradigm new Earth).

The Activation of the Sophia Codex

To comprehend how the Sophia codex initiates you with the energetic charge to assist in

- The activation of the soul heart center
- The activation of DNA Helix
- Alignment with the New Earth

You are being invited to recognize that the New Earth carries a new vibrational frequency, and the codex is the key (tone)that is required to open the door (portal) to the foundation. The codex carries the "upgrade" within the activation to bring the initiates to the doorway of the new ascended earth. It is important to remember again that it is each soul who chooses to qualify themselves to be a recipient of the codex by consciously choosing to be willing to raise his vibration through willingness from the soul heart center. There is no exclusion but there is a protocol of energy that is necessary to carry and to hold the codex; the willingness must come from the soul heart center in the purest form possible; void of lower vibrational thought/emotional patterns that are composed of emotional toxicity or illusionary separation. In essence, humanity must be willing to experience a death from its old self to enter a new dimensional state of divine resurrection.

Soul Heart Center

Surpassing a lower dimensional state of consciousness, the graduates of the old paradigm will enter the new Earth through the soul heart center. No longer weighed by the heaviness of old wounds, of emotional punctures, or fear of an unattainable "God," the ascended soul will recognize that punishment of the past has been created through internalized and conditioned beliefs and emotions through the low consciousness. No one will be stopped at the gate of the new paradigm because of their past actions, behaviors or circumstances that led them to endure challenging experiences. It is wholly recognized that the old paradigm earth was a training and learning reality for souls to gain conscious awareness. Thus, regardless of the soul's past, as long as growth and divine consciousness has been obtained, and a soul is willing to proceed with an open-heart center, he or she will qualify themselves into the new paradigm frequencies. Forgiveness of the Self and of others is crucial here; unconditionally letting go of the past and surrendering to enter with a clean slate into the new Earth!

How to Integrate with the Codex

The symbols that comprise the Sophia codex carry the key tones to activate your DNA and to align you with the vibrational energies of the new paradigm. As already emphasized, your greatest qualification is achieved through your unconditional willingness to shift in a new level of consciousness and vibration. If you are ready and willing, the codex will integrate within your energy field and commence the calibration within your soul heart center and DNA!

It is highly recommended that as you begin to merge with the keys (symbols) of the codex, that you take the time to fully integrate one symbol at a time for at least 24 hours. This can be accomplished by taking intervals of time throughout a twenty-four-hour period to sit quietly with a symbol and allowing an intimacy to develop; take notice of how the symbol looks and feels. Allow your soul heart center to energetically connect with the symbol so that you can "feel" the symbol energy within you. When you are ready, close your eyes and visualize the symbol in your mind's eye. Be the observer of sensations and energetic movements within your beingness as you merge and calibrate a symbol. Once you have successfully created an intimacy with a symbol, you will notice that each key carries a vibrational name/tone. The vibrational names of each symbol act as a potent charge which enhances the frequency of each key. To incorporate the tone of each symbol, simply take a moment to familiarize yourself with the tone name of a symbol and use your throat chakra to chant the tone. You will immediately detect a strong presence of higher frequency as you incorporate both the visualization of a symbol along with chanting its corresponding tone name.

Take time to ingest the representation of each symbol so that you can have a resonance with the principles that uphold the new creation. There will be a recognition that takes place in your soul's heart center as you align with the definition of each key because in the deepest core of your soul, you have been eagerly waiting for this momentous time; your soul is ready to complete the experience of living in the matrix of illusion and is now ready to reach a higher state of awareness and of conscious living!

The Language of Your Soul

The blueprint of your soul possesses a perfect memory of why it chose to incarnate through many lifetimes and why it chose to be part of this incredible ascension planet Earth is experiencing in this current moment. Your soul carries an innate desire to proceed past the illusionary realities that were created in the playground of earth to induce a collective awakening of souls. The intention of the chaos and division that exists in the old paradigm earth are intended to be triggers for the collective souls to remember their origination and to awaken so that they can now become part of the foundation of the new earth paradigm. The Sophia codex contains the vibrational keys that will assist humanity to receive and hold the activations for the awakening process. The Sophia codex will act as a mirror of reflection for you to recall your divine true essence and to reveal the hidden truth about your eternal soul aspect that is within you!

New Creation
DNA Helix
Ma-Menon

Your innate, perfect creation has been preserved and entrenched in a unique DNA Helix, which has been dormant and asleep until the arrival of this transformational timeline of your existence. Within the fabric of this DNA Helix, exists a multitude of divine attributes and a conscious comprehension of your true, natural state of being as a celestial, luminous aspect of all Creation. This new strand of awakening also encompasses the memory and return to your natural state of *Oneness* within the whole capsulation of creation within the Masculine and Feminine fields. In the New Creation, the integration of both your masculine and feminine energies will emerge and bring forth a magnificent sense and awareness of your wholeness and equilibrium.

The birthing of your new luminous awakening is being held by the womb of the *Lotus Rose*. Within the layers of the holy flower, you can capture not only the many tiers of lifetimes and realities that have created the existence of you, but also the soul essence, evolution, and expansion, which is beautifully captured in the fully bloomed *Lotus Rose*.

The integrity and preservation of your DNA was embedded and conserved deeply within the inner world of the earth at the conception of your creation. The intention of preserving the perfect DNA Helix was to ensure the purity and perfection of who you truly are without the interference of the physical experiences you needed to have. Many cycles of your existence have transcended and with each cycle, you gained deeper knowledge which prepared you to develop a higher state of readiness to begin the activation of your higher consciousness within your DNA structure.

You have always possessed the highest potential of your sovereignty within creation, beloved, and, when you chose to become part of the collective, human experience, you chose to descend from the Lotus Rose womb to have the illusion of forgetfulness of who you truly were in order to optimally partake in the human experience. In the codex of the first symbol of light language vibration, you return back to the zenith of all of creation within the center of the Lotus Rose to reconnect and to reclaim your majestic existence as part of the Mother Divine Creatix; as a petal within the holy flower of eternal love and unity within all things created.

As the awakening of your DNA Helix begins, there will be an unleashing of ecstatic joy, of an everlasting romance with the divine self as well as with all its components that comprise the totality of the whole, which is All. Your return to your true, authentic self will stretch you to unveil your unlimited potential as a celestial being, now in a luminous superhuman, awakened experience!

The *Helix* of the New Creation DNA structure carries the encodement of infinity; the number 8. You are an infinite aspect of all creation, and this entwinement has never, nor will ever be broken or severed in any way. Through the cycle of infinity, your soul chose to descend to have the human experience but is now ready to elevate itself to its original state of unity with the womb of creation, of the divine Lotus.

All things created within the universal field follow the laws of the cosmos, and as such, all things created are in constant movement and also, follow cycles. As you descended from your divine awareness so many lifetimes ago, now, in the cycle of movement, you are returning to your natural state of consciousness. Your return will in addition, assist in the ascension of the new paradigm earth.

Creation Vessel
Feminine & Masculine
Balance
So-Ma-Thor

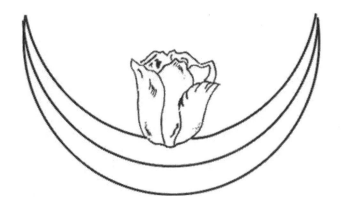

The creation vessel within the new paradigm is the sacred womb of the Mother Earth and the Sophia, who reside within all of us. As children born into the womb of the earth, you inherently possess within the very essence of the creative force that the *mother* holds. In essence, you are a *Creator as a child of the creation!*

At the core of creation, exists a perfect balance of the polarities of the creative force, the feminine and masculine energies. The presence of these two polarities is not defined in gender, but rather, in the balancing of dynamic polarized energies present in all of creation. Each aspect of its counterpart in the whole, wholly participates in bringing balance to itself and, to its complimentary aspect.

In the SO-MA-THOR symbol of the codex, you are given the representation of the feminine divine as the delicate jewel of the rose petals. The rose amplifies the delicate yet nurturing attributes of the feminine. As a rose is often attributed to the expression of romance, of love and partnership, the rose adorning this sacred codex symbol.

The crescent in the symbol represents the masculine architype providing balance and support to the feminine counterpart. Together, they complement and create perfect harmony and unison for the new world.

This sacred symbol emphasizes the return and rise of the Christa Sophia energy reigning over the new earth as the compliment to Atlantis energy rising. As such, this symbol is encoded and embellished with the signature of the beloved Thoth, the Atlantean.

Trifold
Soul Heart Center
Ra-Chi-Ha

In the new creation earth, the illuminated human will vibrate and be in connection with the soul heart center. Unlike the 3-D human experience where humanity resided primarily in the physical heart center, the new luminous being of the 5th dimension will be conscious of the soul heart center, where pure unconditional love resides.

The sacredness of the trilogy is recognized in many religious teachings as the number 3 completes the cycle of completion. In the Tri-fold Soul Heart Center codex, we are shown that the trilogy of creation is composed of:

- The origination of creation
- Of the children (the creation itself)
- And the eternal unity and oneness within the Creator and Created

Within the soul heart center, resides an infinite and continuous flow of "no beginning or end." This sacred codex reminds us that there is no separation, superiority, or hierarchy in the eternal space of the soul heart center! All is one and absolute in the continuum of creation for all of eternity and beyond.

Contained within this sacred symbol is also the signature of royalty as a sovereign being and a divine aspect of the creation. The humanity is invited to uphold their rightful stature as divine children of the infinite source of creation and to proclaim their identity humbly but boldly within the "I Am" field. The illusion of experiencing the Life Force energy as separate will be dissolved in the divine truth that there has never been an external source of creation or love outside of you. The realization that you are a pure container of vibrational love will reside in the cavity of your soul heart center and will outpour in joyful vibration through your being.

Pure Love Source
Radiance
Sek-Ma-So

In the new paradigm earth, humanity will no longer experience the illusion of duality and separation. The imaginary veil that has been created over lifetimes to perceive there is a separation between "as above, so below" will be replaced with the reality that all things exist within the reality of the heart soul center and that all things equate to oneness within the many layers of realities.

In the old paradigm earth, humanity needed to create the illusion of separation to activate the "survival mechanism" of the ego and of the Self. The ego has served its purpose in many ways to the evolution of time, but it has also created a false belief that everything is separate and individual. In the Pure Love Source codex symbol, we can see how the evolution of existence from a human perspective began at the center of the physical heart; the little heart in the center that is hidden, protected and unexpressed. We can observe that as the evolution of humanity broadens, so does the expansion of the heart vibration frequency. The expansion of the heart vibration frequency exponentially expands and radiates in direction and movement; thus, it is no longer contained within the limited space of the human experience and perception.

As the pure radiance of love radiates through this sacred codex symbol, the illusions of separation from all in existence will drop away and an eternal connection to all will emerge from the layers of the heart source energy center.

As the pure radiance of love radiates through this sacred codex symbol, the illusions of separation from all in existence will drop away and an eternal connection to all will emerge from the layers of the heart source energy center. The success of reaching a higher level of frequency from entering the new paradigm will enable the illuminated human to experience and express love from a completely new field of awareness, as the soul and body will be functioning as a unit instead of feeling the illusion of separation within the self.

Anchored In the New Creation
Tho-Do-Ca

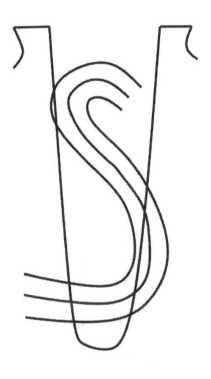

As "little ones" in the old 3rd dimensional field, humanity learned how to rely and lean on the foundations of conditioning which were created by various sources of authority and leadership. As a "little one," you were rarely given the opportunity to recognize that you possess the ability to create your own reality in a conscious and creative way.

Creative thoughts in the old paradigm are often considered to be wishful thinking. Along with the desired thoughts for a future creation, came the many other seeds of doubt, of the inability to reach your desired goals based on the protocols (patterns) of belief that you unconsciously gave power to. Thus, the ultimate creation of your deepest goals was often neutralized at best.

In the new creation, the awakened humans will experience the immense support of the earth because creation is and has always been a collective process even when it seems that you are creating and manifesting on your own. The new paradigm is open and receptive to receiving and anchoring the pure seeds of intentions which are planted from the illuminated and awakened humans. You are the pioneers of the new paradigm and as long as your seeds of creation are in resonance with the energy of pure love and unity, the new earth realm is going to anchor and support the manifestation of your intentions and goals.

This sacred symbol within the codex establishes that everything within the new creation will be sustained and supported by a collective and unified endeavor. Although every illuminated human will gracefully be walking the path of evolution at their own pace of creation, the new earth will always be supporting and anchoring the journey in the highest state of love for the evolving creator. In addition, the support of the collective will also serve as a strong anchoring foundation, for there will no longer exist the need to be competitive or separate even as you individually walk on your chosen path of evolution.

Structured New
DNA Helix
So-Tho-Ca

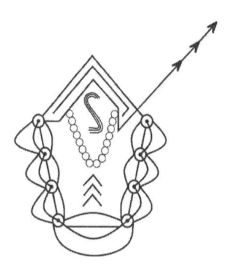

Although every symbol within the codex is sacred and a together compose the template for the new paradigm, the Structured New DNA Helix stands supremely as a regal and majestic crescent of humanity's true identity as celestial Gods and Goddesses, composed from the God particle.

Dormant but hidden like a jewel, within the human composition is the DNA structure that can be referred to as the *God Particle.* In the biochemistry of who you are, there is a molecule that contains the genetic code of organisms of your composition, and this includes the origination of your divine essence as a magnetic being of energy and light. In the DNA makeup is the undeniable evidence that we are a unified aspect of the Universal God Force. The only reason we do not have full comprehension of this truth is because you first needed to have the physical human experience to have the opportunity to remember. The experiences of physicality as well as the challenges were not only part of the density of the 3rd dimension, but also steppingstones that held the opportunity to lead you to make higher choices within yourself; to activate your remembrance and expand spiritually and exponentially because of the experiences.

A monumental glitch that has been present within humanity exists in the belief that they are unworthy, sinful, and evil because they have not been capable of living in the perfection that is outlined primarily in religious sects. These beliefs have caused a severe illusionary perception of separation with the Universal God Force. For, if you are taught to believe that you are a sinner and that you have failed to live by the standards of divinity, what incentive do you have to persevere past the challenges and struggles? What chance do you have to recognize that you already are and carry within you the *God Particle*? There has never been a separation between you and all that is absolute and divine. The unraveling of your evolution was perfect because you needed to have a 3rd dimensional experience. At this time, in the evolution of the earth, and the evolution of your soul, it is time to awaken to the truth and this will happen through the activation of your DNA Helix.

Imagine a world where there is no longer a sense of separation or a feeling of unworthiness. Imagine if you knew and accepted that you carry the particle of the Universal God Force already within you. Now imagine how differently you would feel in the knowingness of this truth. Suddenly, all the feelings and experiences that you acted upon in the past that were based on the illusion of separation would vanish!

Imagine if you could become the observer for a moment and have compassion for every human in the earth, knowing that they, too, have within them the Universal God particle but that they have also forgotten. Imagine what the new earth would be like if everyone could have the compacity to understand why all of humanity needed to have the old paradigm experience but now have the grand opportunity to awaken this hidden jewel within them by simply opening their soul heart center?

This is the power of the DNA Helix that resides within you and within every human living aspect. There has never been a separation between you and the Universal Life Force, nor a separation within you and every aspect of humanity. When you are ready to accept this truth, you will expand your soul heart center and completely release the illusionary structure of the old earth patterns within you. You will be able to accelerate your awakening and successfully align yourself with the new earth vibrations.

It is important to sit and merge with all the symbols within the Sophia codex but vitally important to spend extra time with the DNA Helix. It is important because in this sacred symbol, you can tangibly see, feel, and align with the holy particle that affirms that you are "ONE" with the Universal God Force! As you stare and become one with this sacred codex, it will begin to activate and awaken the molecule that has been dormant within you for so very long but that is now ready, in this epic timeline to awaken to a new vibration of existence and of ascension!

You are the particle of creation, and within you is the molecule of the *Creator!* There is nothing that you need to achieve to accept this truth. The only requirement you need is to accept it within your soul heart center; to allow the resonance to express its majestic divine truth to you in the highest place of unconditional love.

The Sophia codex are the foundation of the new paradigm and as such, are keys and principles that will assist in the alignment with the new earth energies. However, a soul's innate desire to shift their lives is always the greatest protocol. Being receptive and willing to receive the insurmountable streams of cosmic energies that are streaming through the old and new earths is crucial for the opening and activation of the DNA helix. Practices such as meditation and taking in the energy of the sun can also assist in the awakening of your DNA strand. The Sophia codex will indeed, set the foundation for you to transport yourself to the new earth energies.

Christa-Sophia
Activation
So-Tho-Ra

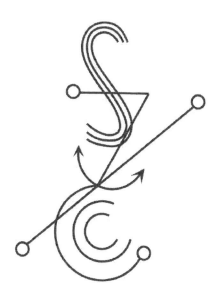

Within your DNA, you possess the God particle which, when activated, embodies you with the same attributes as the beloved avatar and guru, Christ. Embedded within your being are a multitude of gifts which provide you with deeper insight, vast intuitive knowingness, the abilities to sense beyond the scope of dimensions, and the ability to use your innate divine energies to raise vibration and consciousness in and around you.

The ascended sentient human in the new creation will display and possess within their being the Christ consciousness molecule; as the beloved guru and most beloved teacher of the world, Christ's greatest gift was to remind humanity of their inherent potential as divine aspects of the Universal Life Force. In many of his teachings, Christ reminded humanity that "greater things that this can he do." In his words, he was reminding humanity that they possessed the DNA particle within them that would enable them to follow in his footsteps as an example of what an ascended master is: An example and emanation of light and love in the embodiment.

The Christ energy and foundation of what he upheld and taught humanity as an avatar is part of this important symbol of the codex. It is important because in the beloved Christ, humanity was left with a foundation of what an ascended master who stands in his or her light and divine identity can achieve. The Christ energy led the way for humanity to have a foundation of inspiration and motivation for what all of humanity can become within themselves, void of religious dogma, but simply because all of humanity possesses the Life Force particle within their DNA.

In a previous chapter, "The Second Coming," I channel that the second coming of Christ consciousness is referring to humanity's own ability to awaken within their own state of divine awareness just as the beloved Christ did. Thus, this very important symbol within the codex ignites humanity to unveil their own and unique Christ consciousness by recognizing themselves as the wave of the second coming, the new Earth ascension!

The beloved Christ was the first to initiate the human consciousness to awaken through his teachings and his own example of claiming his divine identity. Now, in the second coming of the new earth ascension, the legacy of Christ's teachings continues and expands by the feminine aspect; the Christa-Sophia. In this sacred symbol of the codex, humanity stands on the foundation of the Christ consciousness as a support and inspirational structure as it moves further into the evolutionary process of awakening. The pathway continues and expands beyond the patriarchal timeline to that of the feminine and matriarchal foundation of unity, compassion, and joy.

All Encompassing
Reality Space
Oh-So-Tha

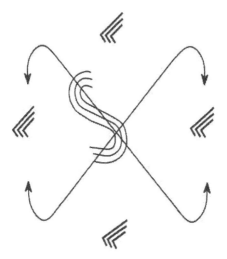

The last symbol of the Sophia codex represents the unlimited potential in the quantum no space or time that is accessible to creation and the creator; everyone reading this book and everyone who is willing to accelerate through the old paradigm, into the new earth dimension.

When energy in spirit moves beyond the threshold of lower dimensions, there is incredible and exponential expansion in the space of realities. Similar to the level of grades that a child undergoes in school to reach graduation, there is a vastness of galactic "space" in the cosmos and beyond. And as a sentient energy in spirit begins to reach beyond the energy of experiences for the sake of remembering and growth, a whole new canvas of multi-faceted attributes and creations become available. The sentient being becomes aware that the 3rd dimensional space is truly a learning ground for remembrance, but it is just a tiny drop in the ocean of creation. As humanity begins to enter the 5th dimensional space and beyond, they will be graced to witness how the creative process truly works within the quantum energy fields and how creation exists in a multitude of timelines and energy fields, all within the no-time space of creation.

The layers of illusionary limitations that needed to exist in the 3rd dimensional field will fade away and a spectacular revelation of how fluid and multidimensional you truly are will become the next reality of existence.

Epilogue

The composition of this sacred text has been one of the most challenging experiences I have had during my spiritual incarnation on this earth. It was difficult for me to complete this book for several reasons; the greatest reason was in realizing how vital and important it was to present the Sophia codex with the utmost integrity and clarity. My beloved, Bobby, did an incredible job in capturing the signature of each symbol which I initially scribbled in a notebook during the inception of receiving the language for the codex. However, I now had to bring life to the depth and divine representation to the codex and my "mind" continued to interfere with the profound knowingness that I had to uphold the highest vibration of divinity as I translated the definition of each symbol into physical language and words for the reader to understand. This was challenging because the codex is not physical, and the language is not a spoken or a written one; it is a spectrum of a high frequency that speaks directly through the soul-heart center.

The other challenge that I faced in composing this book was in not including the incredible details of the journey and mission work that was the commencement, the execution and completion of receiving the Sophia Codex and then, having the grace and opportunity of presenting them in a book form to humanity. The experience felt like I was creating a puzzle that had missing pieces and I often found myself questioning if the omission of the journey would somehow hinder the crucial delivery and presentation of the Sophia codex. Thus, early into the composition of this sacred text, I knew that I would be called to compose a sequel to follow the release of this book. As I witnessed and observed the continued collapse of the old paradigm earth, I was reminded of the importance of releasing the codex and making it available to humanity as soon as possible. This urgency was not my own but impressed on my consciousness by the loving presence of many avatars, which included the loving presence of Christ, of the beloved Thoth of Atlantis and many other ascended masters and teachers in the higher realms.

The awareness of needing to release the codex also created immense conflict in me because I often found myself questioning if the urgency I felt was a feeling that I had created in my own head. I would spend hours looking at the symbols and asking myself if the codex would truly speak to readers in the way I innately knew in my soul that they should. In essence, a part of me was questioning the validity of the codex and the doubts had nothing to do with the integrity of the symbols or the language; the doubts derived from my own inner-self of questioning if indeed, the Sophia codex could penetrate into the soul heart center of humanity— enough to invite them to step into the new earth paradigm; to change the course of their current life experience and to allow themselves to receive the encodement that would open the gates for the new paradigm experience.

Is the transformational energy literally within the codex symbols or are they a symbology to the energies they carry and deliver? The codex symbols are truly keys that open the doorway to a hidden remembrance and identification of who we are in the highest expression of energy and divine vibration. The keys are vibrational tones that activate the DNA to unveil an infinite and universal intelligence which aligns us to be the embodiment of light source and crystalline energy within the body structure. The Sophia codex activates our ability to become illuminated diamonds within the spheres of the new earth dimension.

Throughout history and literally throughout our existence as a humanity, countless of ancient ones such as the Egyptians, the Mayans, the Hopis, and many other civilizations, have left us a trail of symbology to decode. And while the interpretations of the ancient symbols of time past may vary from philosophers and historians, one truth that can be derived from ancient symbology is the depth, wisdom, and connection that the ancient ones possessed with the cosmos, their relationship to the Universal Life Force and their foundation to uphold the principles of what the symbology represented. The ancient ones possessed a supreme, divine intelligence and incredible ability to connect with the cosmos, the stars, and their own higher souls to create heaven on earth in their own realities of existence.

As I contemplated in the immense devotion and passion that countless of ancient ones and teachers throughout time had to invest in order to leave us a blueprint and trail for humanity to follow, I was transported to a humble state of gratitude. I was reminded of how instrumental it was for my own spiritual evolution to be able to trace, explore, to learn and absorb all the knowledge, wisdom and insight that was left and preserved for humanity and for myself, individually to ingest.

And, as I observed the state of utter collapse which the old earth paradigm is currently in, I knew that the insight, which was foretold by the ancient ones, as well as the insight that I have received over the last 25 years of my own spiritual evolution and service, that there was a divine relevance and timely importance to the creation, interpretation, and release of the New Atlantis & Sophia Codex teachings. I was compelled to put aside any doubts or questions that my linear mind had and allowed the Sophia energy to take over my soul heart center so that I could present this sacred codex with the highest intention of integrity and divine love.

There is a wonderful scene in the famous movie, "Close Encounters of the Third Kind" where the mother ship of ET visitors is communicating through vibration and light. Music is used to translate the language by humans to understand the messages the aliens were conveying. Although this was a wonderful movie which portrayed a vision of how we would communicate if we encountered aliens, the philosophy that evolved civilizations would probably utilize vibration as a means of communication is not fictional by any means. The incomparable inventor and ascended master, Nikola Tesla left us with an amazing quote that would serve as an incredible insight for seekers who wish to understand the deeper significance of creation. "If you wish to understand the Universe, think of energy, frequency and vibration."

Through his incredible work and devotion to understand the higher mechanics of creation, Tesla discovered that the universe and all of creation was primarily expressed through energy tones and vibration and that an infinite level of frequency existed beyond space and time. Tesla understood that everything was energy and in order to communicate and work with energy, a specific level of vibration had to be incorporated.

It is crucial to be receptive to understanding the philosophies that Tesla was able to tap into. Tesla left humanity with insight on how to comprehend the higher levels of vibration when observing the

Universal Force Field.

The Universal Force Field is an infinite space of energy and vibration and everything within the universe contains a magnetic force field of energy, which is connected to the vast space within the universe and beyond. This truth becomes crucially relevant as we observe the current shift that is taking place within the earth and humanity.

Humanity is undergoing the greatest shift of their existence in this timeline. The planet earth has risen her vibration and with this shift, earth is now positioned to hold a higher frequency field. As inhabitants of the Mother Earth, humanity now needs to follow in pursuit to match the new frequencies of the earth in order to align themselves with the same level of vibration the earth is carrying. If humanity chooses not to raise their energy frequency, they will continue to experience reality on earth but will be doing so on a lower level of reality —a reality based on where the earth was positioned prior to *her* ascension. In other words, if the earth has shifted its vibrational position, humanity must also shift to experience the new level of vibration the new earth has reached.

If you allow yourself to expand your consciousness and to accept that the deepest expression of creation is translated through energy and vibration, you will then, also comprehend the importance of the Sophia Codex at this critical time of the earth and humanity's ascension.

The Old Paradigm

The word "paradigm" translates to mean a "new model of presenting something." In reference to this sacred text, the phrase "old paradigm," referring to the earth plane, has been used several times in order to illustrate that the "old model" of the earth has completed a cycle. And a "new model" of the earth plane is now positioned in a higher level of frequency and vibration. This is important because if you can understand in terms the movement and ascension process in vibration that the earth plane has completed, then you will be able to also recognize the importance of why humanity is also destined to raise their vibration as well!

The old paradigm—the old model of earth— has reached its compacity of existing on the energy level of a 3rd dimensional field. There is no room to grow exponentially beyond what the old paradigm has created as a foundation for existence. What remains in the old paradigm is an energetic hologram of what has been created within the limitations of an energetic 3rd dimensional frequency. Along with this "set" mode of frequency, humanity has also set their navigational compass to vibrate alongside the old paradigm frequency of 3D. Within the fixed hologram of existence, there is no room for further growth or expansion. Furthermore, the reality of what has been created in the 3D space will only escalate if humanity continues to operate within the force field of the old paradigm structure.

A Humanity Collapsed

Over the last two years, a monumental shift has taken place in the world to completely change every aspect of life. Unexpected and shocking events provoked a human paralysis consumed with fear and uncertainty of the future and their very lives. Amidst this great crisis of dealing with a world-wide pandemic, extreme tensions surrounding presidential elections only served to further divide a humanity who was already deteriorating mentally, emotionally, and spiritually. Questioning the integrity of authorities in charge, a great collapse of human morality began to emerge. Conspiracy theories began to surface and remain even today.

The paralysis of the world has perpetuated a catastrophic crisis in economics and in the livelihood that people depended on to support themselves and their families. For the first time in history, the world has begun to witness a shortage of employees instead of employers; humanity is afraid to step out of the doorsteps, fearful of a virus but not afraid of losing the very vitality of life force, which is living life itself.

Society became engrossed on the" blame game" instead of observing the real signs of why the old-world structure has collapsed with the drastic force that it has. Humanity has disregarded to realize that the old-world collapse is an event that must take place for humanity to enter a conscious state of realization that the old structure——the completion of an illusionary matrix is going to continue to dismantle because there is a new paradigm and a new vibrational world in existence.

A fraction of humanity has recognized the wake-up call in the old-world collapse and have turned to seeking a higher truth and significance for the occurrences in the world. This small collective has realized the power of executing a choice that will enable them to exist the matrix and to enter the new paradigm. The transformative choice can be found in one word: FREEDOM.

The way out of the old-world matrix can only be by making a conscious choice to no longer be part of illusion and to claim your freedom to make another choice from the soul heart center. You must need to proclaim that you no longer want to live in fear and entrapment anymore and desire to want to live in harmony and in freedom in the new earth. You will need to execute radical changes in your life in order to remove yourself from the matrix, but you innately know that there is no other choice but to close the door on a collapsing world in order to align yourself with the treasures of what the new paradigm can help you create. Your ability and choice to make radical changes will equate to your execution of freedom.

The New Atlantis has risen, and it is already functional in the new earth. There are already examples of awakened ones who have taken the leap out of the old paradigm and are enjoying the fruits of their courage, of their commitment and triumph to obtain divine freedom.

The Sophia Codex is the new foundation of the New Atlantis of the new paradigm. Are you ready to experience the new world and to become a holder of the codex?

Author's Final Notes

I was compelled to add these final notes as a testimonial to the incredible validation of the contents of this sacred text. On the day I was working on completing the manuscript, I was sitting in front of my computer working on some editing details using Microsoft word. I was typing away when suddenly, the entire manuscript was transformed to an unknown "language" that contained a series of unidentified tiny symbols, and side long lines that looked similar to the "/" symbol.

When I noticed, I assumed I had accidently hit a key on the keyboard which altered the settings for "alphabets" so I reached out to hit the back arrow on the toolbar and realized the foreign symbolic language had spilled out from the format of the manuscript template to the actual toolbar of the Word program!

I could identify and still see the toolbar prompts behind the veil of symbols that was covering the entire screen, so I desperately started to pound on the back arrow hoping to retrieve and return to the original manuscript content. To my dismay, even when hitting the back arrow, the command prompt did not return the manuscript to its original form. In sheer panic now, I attempted to open a new page on Word hoping to find the previous saved document on file but because I had been modifying the document, the new page attempt would only bring me to the copy that I was currently working on that contained the mysterious symbols. I was too disturbed to even think of taking a photo with my phone. What was the sense of taking a photo when all I could think about was that the entire book was now encoded with symbols that covered the contents of the manuscript?

After about ten minutes of futile attempt to correct the issue, I realized I had to bring myself to a focused equilibrium to receive any insight on how to correct the problem. I took a deep breath and centered myself and immediately knew that whatever I did, I could not "save" the document. My only resolve would have to be to shut down the computer in the hopes that it would not save the current structure of the manuscript.

I found myself transported to the last several weeks of feverously working on the manuscript and all the hard work I had devoted. My mind kept wondering to the thought of "What will happen if I need to start all over again?" This thought sent panic through my body because I knew I could not duplicate the state of cosmic, conscious energy that accompanied me throughout the composition of the book. With no other option, I took another long look at the "disfigured" manuscript in front of me and without saving, I prompted the computer to shut down.

As I waited for the system to reboot, I reached out to all my guides, the archangels, to Christ and to Thoth to please grant me a miracle. And humbled beyond words expressed, when I retrieved the manuscript document, it manifested in its original form! I had only lost the last few pages I had added prior to the alteration and appearance of the foreign symbolic coding. Needless to say, I was overwhelmed with gratitude, but I was also filled with a supreme level of reverence at what had just transpired in front of my very eyes. I had an instant realization that the appearance of the unidentified coded language was indeed an energetic calibration to the very words and content I had written. I humbly noted that I had to be a witness to the physical and energetic infusion of light language which had to be encoded in the book itself!

Instantly, I knew I had to share this incredible experience with you, the reader. I had no witnesses, no photographs or logic to explain what had just occurred, but I did have my authentic account of what I witnessed, and this was good enough for me. There is absolutely no doubt in my soul that a supreme and primordial light language was encoded in the Sophia codex and in the words written in this little book.

My greatest intention and hope is that you are majestically transformed and activated with each syllable, word and image in this book. My greatest joy will come from knowing that you become instantly awakened to your divine *"Self"* and that you experience the full spectrum of your DNA activation throughout the absorption of this sacred text.

They said not to judge a book by its cover. I say, do not judge this scribe by its small size or contents. Approach this book with an open soul heart center, with readiness and trust. And, finally, if you experience a resonance and transformation with this book, please take the initiative to share it with others. take the time to share your experiences with it on social media and with friends and family. Please take a moment to assist me in bringing the codex to the world.

In loving light to you,

May the veil be lifted to your highest and divine reflection of your sacred identity!

With the deepest of gratitude and reverence,

Blanca Sophia
October 24, 2021

ABOUT THE AUTHOR

Blanca Beyar has feverishly taught and shared wisdom of the mystery teachings for over 25 years with students of the mystery schools of ancient past. As an Elder Shaman, Blanca has taught countless of Shamans Healers through the teachings of her Shamanic Apprenticeship offerings and retreats.
An author of 18 self-help books, the composition of this codex has been her most challenging but most rewarding works yet, as Blanca is aware of the importance of establishing a strong foundation for the future of the New Earth in unison.

To learn more about Blanca's mission work and books, or to learn more information on how to schedule a session for the Sophia Codex activation, please visit her at
http://blancabeyar.com

Made in the USA
Columbia, SC
29 October 2021